The wonderful
of
Walter

CW00404905

Copyright

First publish 2021 by Derren Riley
ISBN: 978-1-3999-0846-7

Copyright Derren Riley 2021.

The author's rights are fully asserted. The right of Derren Riley to be identified as the author of this work has been asserted according to the Copyright, Design and Patents Act 1988.

All rights reserved. No part of this publication may be reproduced, stored in a retrieval system or transmitted in any form without prior permission of the copyright owner.

Acknowledgements

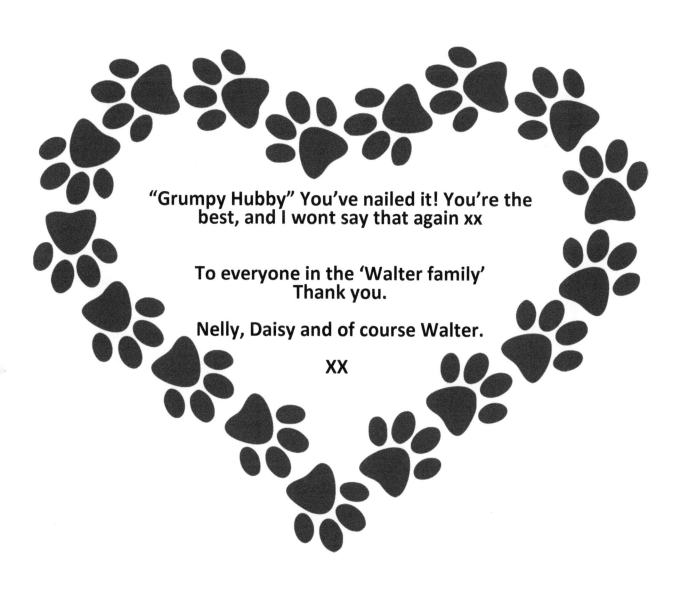

"Grumpy Hubby" You've nailed it! You're the best, and I wont say that again xx

To everyone in the 'Walter family'
Thank you.

Nelly, Daisy and of course Walter.

xx

Preface:-

The adventures continue. Sometimes you want the Ferris wheel to stop turning but with the "Lanky legged racing machine" Walter, I doubt it ever will. The story of the feral dog is chronicled in "Walter", book one and "Walter, life is an adventure." book two. They tell the story of how one special dog, not only captured everyone's heart, but also how he bought a little town together. As time progressed the pebble and ripple effect has spread far and wide and Walter is synonymous across the country.

With the support of his canine siblings Nelly and Daisy the "Three Amigos" live life on the edge and drag everyone else with them. One thing I have learnt though is - If you don't live on the edge you can't see the view and its definitely a view worth seeing.

Thank you Wonderful Walter xx

The wonderful world of Walter

Walters 'Tail'.

Daisy and I are huddled together as the Boiler has broken and Mum said we have no hot water or heating.... I didn't realise what that meant until I came back from the beach and I had to have a cold shower. I created enough fuss that Dad put the kettle on and boiled me a bucket to dip my feet in and now I'm relaxing as close to the fire as I can get. Apparently we need a part and can't get it until tomorrow, so I'm going to bed soon.

Mum cooked dinner and it was awful.... Dad put it in the bin and is now filling up on cheese and biscuits .... our favourites. Not sure where Mums gone but she's not happy.

If the heating isn't working tomorrow Mum I'm leaving. Despite having a hot water bottle, a wool blanket and Teddy bear bedding, I am frozen.

Normal service has resumed.... We are warm.

Thanks Mum for getting the heating going. We do actually know it was the man who turned up in his little red van who did it, but nevertheless we are now happy.

She always has to be the centre of attention

Coffee is served

I finished work at 1pm after a long morning. I was late to bed last night as I was out trekking around some very muddy field in a very dodgy area, looking for a runaway dog. Torch in hand and eyes peeled I found no sign of him. Eventually falling into bed Walter made it quite clear he was not happy I'd been out. He has now taken to sleeping under the covers, including his head and has to be touching me only problem being if I move he grunts, I have to remain still...

He was panting a lot, then suddenly leapt off the bed barking at the window (no idea why) in the melee he frightened Nelly who promptly weed all over the quilt... great it was brand new on Monday and by Thursday it will be in the dry cleaners!

Bed stripped, quilt changed and back to sleep. NO! Walts wants a wee 3:57am (my digital clock again) out in the garden we go ... lots of stars, very clear night and he is just ambling around and smelling the flowers ... "Hurry up Walts".

Back in bed 4:16am and then alarm at 5:30. Great nights sleep!

Good News though the little dog was found this morning so I came home in a great mood and it rubbed off on the gang. We had an amazing walk, met lots of nice people and I was feeling happy. We stopped for a hot chocolate in our favourite place, the waiter tried not to have eye contact in the hope we wouldn't stop at his restaurant but it didn't work.

Next as we were in no rush, we went to see our friend at the opticians but unfortunately she was busy but we still raided the biscuits, one for each Amigo. Across the road to the estate agent to see another one of our friends and then OMG it began....

My Mum and Dad bought me a little table for my lounge in the shape of stacked books (I fell in love with it ages ago) unfortunately it didn't arrive in time for Christmas but is due very soon. Good idea, or so I thought I will just pop in the shop and see if there is any news on it. The shop is beautiful with very expensive suites, tables, lamps and artefacts God knows what possessed me to take the gang in there. I opened the door and the look of horror descended on the owners face. He virtually hurdled across furniture to prevent me getting too far into the shop. He explained my table would arrive Saturday and then tried to make conversation by saying what beautiful well behaved dogs. At this Walter wagged his long thin tail and promptly knocked over a bowl of fruit that was precariously balanced on top of a glass shelf. In my effort to stop it breaking I made the situation worse, the plastic fruit inside the bowl rolled along the floor.... Great a ball thought Nelly as an imitation apple rolled past her nose.... "leave" I said which she did only for me to bend down pick it up just as Daisy decided enough was enough she needed a lie down on the settee.... why me and why my gang?

I have asked my hubby to go and collect the table, I daren't go in there again and as for the poor owner he doesn't want us to…

We are home now and the gang are resting or rather all out for the count....

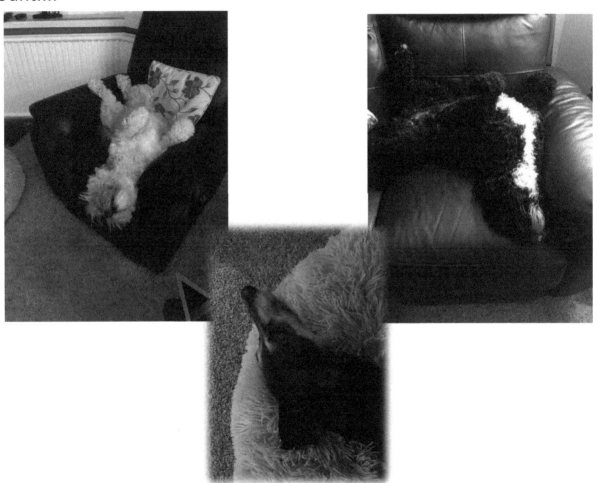

I love you so much Daisy

Shop lifter!

What a beautiful day it's been. We set off in the sunshine and completed the whole walk before storm whatever his name set in!

Yesterday we walked a short walk in torrential rain in new waterproof boots and guess what they leaked ,soaked my feet, wet my socks that rubbed my ankles and gave my humungous blisters on my heels, so today was back to my faithful wellies, compeed plasters and a slow pace ... it's been lovely. We walked the very muddy woods, but we didn't care. All three happy little beans. Walter and Daisy in the bushes and racing about like maniacs, Nelly close by waiting for me to constantly throw her ball. Along Fairlawn where we met an Alsatian who just wanted to play but Walts was unsure, however eventually he got into the swing of things and they had a good run around. Daisy was not impressed so took her frustration out on Nelly by biting her ear and running off with her ball... she is evil. We stopped for a hot chocolate and a catch up with our lovely friend Sue and savoured the sunshine and a peaceful sit down BUT that was all about to change. Sue wanted to go in the pet shop, oh no that's like taking a tribe of naughty children into a sweet shop. I'm sure whilst Sue and I were drinking our hot chocolates the Amigos were concocting a plan!... "Nelly you keep her occupied, then you distract her Daisy and I'll grab the treats and share them with you when we get outside"!!!!

So, Nelly tried to steal a salmon flavoured bone (she hates salmon) whilst telling her off Daisy grabbed a pigs ear .... put that down -Please don't make me touch it.... in the meantime Walter was filling himself up with Biscuit shaped lamb things @ 39p each ... it was only when the assistant tried to grab it did I realise what was happening. Unfortunately she was too slow and Walter swallowed it straight down .... so much for sharing, Nelly and Daisy are refusing to speak to him tonight.

I can't believe he was shop lifting so blatantly.

Back across the park which is more like a swimming pool and home. Hot shower and relax.... I have a little seat in my kitchen that was made for me to sit on in the middle of the night when the dogs need a wee and I'm waiting for them to come in, today it was Daisy's sunshine seat.

Travellers Tale.

We set off this morning enveloped in a cloud of mist. Very chilly but beautiful.

We headed out to sea which is a little disconcerting when you turn around and can see absolutely nothing. The closer we got to the water the mist was lifting but behind us was a thick blanket. The gang had a ball racing around happy and so was I.

The sun came out and there was warmth in it, absolutely fabulous.

So Regal

Chuck it then!

What have you found Daisy?

Walking back towards the shore we met a family of 'settled travellers' (their words).... the man was extremely interested in Walter and was asking me loads of questions but I remained a little guarded. He told me I'd devalued him by having him castrated – good! (he's not for sale). He said he was obviously fed well, in other words he is FAT- good! (can't run as fast). He then said how old is he? I explained we found him and we thought about 5. He called Walter over to him (Walts wary of some men but not this one, I guess he must be ok) over he went. The man stroked him then rolled his lip back and said NO WAY was Walts 5, 3 Max " Good 15 years left in him yet" he said ... OMG I'll be nearly 75. I can't keep this pace up for 15 years!!!

Telling me to keep him safe he bid me farewell and walked away.

I need a lie down.

Bed Bug!

Remember in the beginning when this lanky legged racing machine was frightened of his own shadow ... Oh boy NOT any more ... too scared to walk on the laminate floor, now slides across them like Eddy the Eagle in pursuit of Daisy. Scared to be left on his own (even though the girls were still here) not anymore, now cocky enough to open cupboard doors and help himself to biscuits and crisps.

Wary of the stairs but now three at a time to see who can get in bed first and that is where the trouble begins. Obviously he has legs that do not tuck away in a neat little shape so 3 dogs on the bed leaves very little room. However brainwave by me (or so I thought) as long as Walter can touch me he sleeps well, so I bought a draft excluder to put down the middle of the bed as a kind of dividing line.... for 2 nights it was fantastic. His head resting on the sausage shape excluder and he slept. The girls on Walters side too .... I had room. However last night it all went pear shape. With fireworks going off fidgety Walter dives under the covers for safety and guess what he foiled my plan. He slid under the draught excluder and rested his head on my stomach with his legs pinning me down. I'm goosed now as the sausage was ceremonially dumped on the floor and all 3 dogs climbed in bed with me .... looks like I'm back to a 6 inch square.

Good bye storm Ciara hello Storm Dennis

Yesterday we, the three Amigos and me tackled the beach at Lytham. We tried on Monday but that was impossible as the sea was smashing against the railings however yesterday the sun was shining and life was … calm.

We set off through the woods extremely muddy and very very slippy but eventless then along Fairlawn where we met a lovely couple who remembered the tale of Walter but knew nothing of him since his capture. The lady was enthralled and kept hugging him. As always Walter took it in his stride.

Down the beach and WOW it looked like a battle ground. Lots of dead birds ... Daisy in heaven, boats washed up on the path and some smashed to bits. All a new adventure playground for the gang, the best bit of all was a tree that had almost made it to shore. The gang loved wading out to it and then climbing aboard like they were on a raft... Obviously Daisy was the main explorer with Walter a close second and Nelly more interested in her ball, nothing new there.

Close Call.

Today was down the main beach as I was off work, so checked the tide times and off we went. Absolutely deserted.... heaven!.... unleashing the gang and setting off I realised I'd left Nelly's ball in the car... do I carry on regardless as it was quite a hike back or do I look at her little face begging me to throw the ball i don't have, DAMN.... come on guys we need to go back to the car. Walter smiling as he thought the walk was over and he could get back to the radiator came straight away and Daisy basically said S** off and kept running but in the wrong direction... come on Nell let's go and get your "ball" at that word she was over like a shot.... walking the opposite direction to Daisy she was at my side like a rocket especially when the treats came out. Back to the car grabbed the ball and off we go again. Heading out to sea Walter crying all the way as he was cold. Daisy running about trying to bite his legs and Nelly chasing her ball.. the wind

picked up and I think storm Dennis was letting us know he wasn't too far away. Looking at the clouds it suddenly went very dark I think we need to head back before the rain sets in.... great timing 3 dogs back in the car and wham! The heavens opened....we were lucky.

You STINK.

If only I could transfer the smell of this dog or rather these dogs, yes Daisy and Walter on to this page. Trust me you lot wouldn't want him then.

Sun shining not sure where Dennis went but he's not in LYTHAM thank goodness so we set off for our daily constitutional. Through the woods gosh! it was busy lots of dogs but no issues. Walter chasing a few spaniels giving off his deadly death rumble but all in fun and came back immediately I blew my whistle. Daisy met up with the love of her life Bertie a spaniel and seem to spend a considerable amount of time in the bushes with him ... she is such a floozy.

Nelly stuck with me...

Down the front where we met a Bassett hound, how lively was he. Walter and him had a grand old time chasing each other about, Daisy was not impressed so bit Nelly's ear to try and make her chase her, no chance.

Down the beach and why oh why does Walter have the homing instinct for all dead vile critters... released from his lead, nose in the air and he was off closely followed by his side kick in pink pyjamas ....

As the offending thing was on the waters edge I did not venture out to see what it was but kept walking with Nelly and throwing her ball... she's an angel.

I kept turning around but all I could see were Walter's legs in the air ... this was going to be messy.

Eventually they returned and OMG they absolutely stank and were dripping in white blubber (hope your not eating).

No hot chocolate stop for us on the way home, no way could I subject anyone to this smell even I felt sick.

Daisy obviously realized that the smell was not too pleasant and tried desperately to wipe her face and shoulders on my legs great, we all stink now.

Home hot shower and shampoo in the garden... Walter Freezing and shivering like a jelly but serves him right. Nelly quick wash of her feet and inside she can go the other two scrubbed to within an inch of their lives and me clothes off once again in the garden .... my poor neighbours! Everything on a hot wash in the washing machine. In the meantime my son thought it would be hilarious to lock the back door go out the front and take his girlfriend for lunch, how nice I hear you say .... Not when all your clothes are in the washing machine in an outside utility room and

you are stood in your bra and knickers. I phoned him to please come home and let me in but he laughed and left me stranded. Oh well head up and stroll around to the front door with Walter and Daisy In tow praying nobody's around .... phew! We made it .... Another day in the life of RILEY.

Tell tales...

Do you remember when you were at school and there was always one person who snitched on you for something. That is Daisy!

We went down the beach today. Cold, windy as anything and empty - beautiful. Nelly a happy little bean, Walter a lively little bean and Daisy the snitch. Every time Walter chased her she belted back to me tripping me over on one occasion and letting me know in no uncertain terms that Walter was bullying her. After a severe telling off Walter ran and left Daisy on her own Oh no! she wasn't having any of that and off she ran after him.... what a pain. Nelly and I just watched the scenario unfold.

Come on Daisy

Keep up Walts!!

Once we hit the sea the sea birds were out In abundance and the naughty two were in full flight after them... me and Nells just paddled but how happy were we.

Drum Roll ....

Today has all been about Walter. Obviously I think he's an Uber special dog and I believe you all think the same.

I absolutely adore Nelly and Daisy but Walter has a quality I can't put my finger on.

Let's go back to the book signing of book two in our local department store. A lady came into the shop pushing her Mum in a wheel chair (her mum had dementia) she stopped to look at my book and her mum just sat head down looking into her own little world. Without realising what Walter was doing he placed his head in her lap and she rested her hand on his head and smiled. Her daughter was so shocked and said her mum never smiled anymore she was quite emotional. That got me thinking... could Walter actually help other people, like people have helped him. I applied to "Pets as therapy" and began the procedure. Each stage we passed culminating with his full on assessment this morning at Preston North-end Football club and he has passed with flying colours. In fact the assessor said he has eyes into my soul.... this dog is very special.

Walter is now able to officially go into schools, hospitals and nursing homes, in fact anywhere where he can spread a little happiness. Walts you star.

And relax....

Haha! In this house you have got to be joking. Up early no reason just couldn't sleep may have had something to do with the fact Walts was laying across my chest and I could neither breath nor move. Anyway it culminated with me getting up.

ha ha ha - "I squashed her "

Hubby informed me it was due to rain all afternoon so perhaps it might be best to walk early, in other words clear off.

Everyone happy and not raining yet and then Daisy, damn devil dog Daisy caught a squirrel. It screamed, I screamed, Walter stood there as much as to say I am a therapy dog I am a gentle being and Nelly was somewhere with her ball.

Unfortunately the little thing wasn't dead so what could I do. I couldn't leave it for some other dog to rip to bits so I carefully picked it up and put it in the bag I carry poo bags and balls in. I actually felt sick. Daisy was leaping in the air to get at it so I shortened the strap so it was high up on my chest then I thought what if it has a rush of adrenaline and leaps out of my bag and rips my throat out, I carefully removed the bag from around my neck at which point the squirrel appeared to stop breathing. I walked to the end of the woods and lifted the little thing out of my bag and examined it closely even putting my ear to its nose to see if it was breathing ... nothing I then buried it in a poo bag and placed it in the bin. It really upset me and Daisy wasn't impressed either.

The rest of the walk was issue free although there were two swans resting on the beach I categorically refused to let Daisy off until we were well away from them. No way would they fit in my little bag.

As hubby said the rain set in this afternoon so a spot of baking was on the cards. I am going to a dementia fund raising night tomorrow and it's bring a cake. My cooking skills are zilch (example I made a lamb stew a few years ago and instead of putting fresh rosemary from the garden I put a fir tree branch, looked the same to me ... family not impressed) however I made meringues.... perfect, in fact marvellous. Leaving them in the oven to cool down until tomorrow.

Why Oh why can I not just be left alone.... hubby has had the oven on pre heat for the past 15 mins for the meal he has cooked us and guess what he has burnt my b******y meringues I'm so mad and all he can do is laugh.

Another fun filled day in the RILEY house hold (RIP little squirrel).

Let's just go Mum

Junkie ...

I know you are going to struggle with this but we've had a very eventful walk today.

I don't work Mondays but I have to today but on my terms. Obviously my gang come first and as the sun was shining I thought I'd take them to the beach and then go to work this afternoon. All togged up and in the car, Nelly sang the whole way ... what a noise.

Opening the boot was like releasing Exocet missiles only fortunately they were all strapped in.... this will be fun.

Walter was extremely bouncy and as soon as I let him loose he was off. My eyesight isn't the best but he was legging it towards what looked like the Lochness monster, closely followed by the other two. When I finally caught them all up it was a tree branch stuck in the sand ... no monster but nevertheless great for weeing against.

Throwing the ball for Nelly everyone happy then I lobbed the ball just as Walter raced into its line of fire, I hit him in his rib cage and he screamed and collapsed in a heap. Both Nelly and Daisy raced to me and I tried(I can't run due to a stiff leg) but hobbled rapidly towards the injured soldier... obviously he has been watching football with my son over the weekend as it was basically a dive... quick rub and he was fine... the initial noise sounded like I'd shot him... in the meantime Daisy was foraging and OMG she ran up to me with a syringe and needle in her mouth... trying to stay calm and praying Walter wouldn't leap on her I ask her to drop it.... but off she ran. Sitting on the sand, (wet sand I add) I really was

panicking. She came back to see why I was sitting down and I produced a sausage from my bag much more tasty than a junkies needle (whole empty beach and she finds this).

Picking the thing up I carefully put it in my bag to dispose of later. My daughter phoned just after the melee and said "mum you need to ring the vets, she might have AIDS" .... straight on the phone. I've checked her mouth as best I could but can see no marks and we will just keep an eye on her. Why me Why???

Deciding enough was enough we turned round to walk back to shore and now I'm relaxing at work... well I can't at home!

Another day in paradise.....

I hate this outfit

Angel Dog Nelly – not!

You look at Nelly and think how cute, ha! How wrong can you be. Nelly barks at every single minuscule noise and she drives us totally nuts. The fact we are now at home with her and the other two 24/7 has only enhanced her diva status and now if you 'dare' to ignore her she howls incessantly until she receives the attention she feels she deserves.

Why should you stay in bed even though you can't go to work well with Nelly you can't. 5:45am she stands at the side of the bed and does what I like to call her night howl it's a muffled version of the hound of the

Baskerville. Walter snuggles further under the quilt so he can't hear her, Daisy refuses to sleep with us at all and prefers to find an empty bedroom.

Not sure what today has in stock but I'm sure it will include cleaning oh and doggie cuddles in abundance ....

I have noticed over the past week that Mum is either cleaning everything with a toothbrush and bleach or putting 'stuff' in the washing machine... I'm not moving for fear of either.

You've got to hand it to Walter

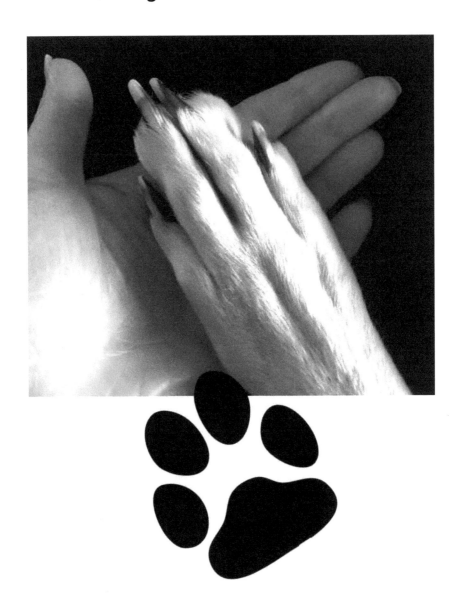

'Thistle' be the day.

My kids are 23 & 24 so yes my days of being constantly badgered are long gone or so I thought until I had Daisy...

Having spent the past 2 weeks scrubbing my house to within an inch of its life with bleach and a toothbrush the pace can finally slow down a bit and with my kids choosing to live with their other halves it may actually stay clean although I think I'd like to see them.

With the sun shining and Walter a little more perky than he has been we set off for the woods. Not a sole about, absolutely beautiful and then a little rabbit decided to pop its head out of a bush and say hello. Nelly having been bought up with bunny's was nonplussed and just kept walking, Walter to be fair wasn't too interested until Daisy, yes Devil Dog Daisy virtually did a back flip through the bushes to rip its little head off.... with me screaming "Run Bun" Nelly laying in the dirt and Daisy and Walter entangled in the brambles it was chaos. Now Daisy being only small could quite easily untangle herself but Walter was well and truly stuck.... waving 'finest' out of date sausages didn't work he was trapped and beginning to panic.... Great!... Daisy definitely didn't help the situation as she was running backwards and forwards through the under growth but Walts was trapped by a lasso of thistles. Only one thing for it I had to wade in. Bending is not in my remit due to a wonky leg but funny what you can do when you have to. Laying on my tummy I commando rolled into the Bush... Thank God nobody was about. Tying the leads around the thistles I was able to pull them above his head and trapping the bottom thistles with my legs I was able to make a hole big enough for him to climb through... Nelly was still sitting in the dirt waiting ... Daisy thought this was a great game and kept leaping all over me. Trying to get up wasn't easy especially as I had stung my hands on stinging nettles... it's a weird prickly feeling and no I couldn't find a doc leaf.

Trudging home and let me sit down. NO chance. Sun bed and stretch out oh NO Nelly with her head through the arm of the chair pulling on my pocket... then punching me to move and finally laying side ways on across my neck to so my breathing is restricted I give in..... Dinner time.

Pains Staking Walk.

Yes it is us again after ANOTHER fun filled afternoon ...

In the woods and once again it's deserted. The beautiful thing about the lock down is the wild life that is daring to come out during the day however the cheeky bunny that we saw yesterday and caused so much chaos was back again today only this time it had a strategy and unfortunately Walter came off worst.

Everything was going great all three happily sniffing, cocking (well Walts was) and chasing balls when suddenly and I'm going to call him Rodger rabbit popped his head out of a hole and belted down the path in front of us... Walter was in close pursuit of Daisy who was in the lead and Nelly couldn't be a*****

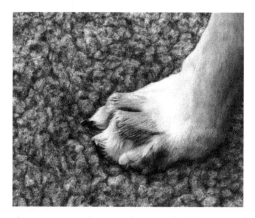

(bothered) the rabbit raced through the undergrowth and made it through the railings into the safety of the school field and I swear it was laughing as Walter screamed and fell to the floor. OMG... now what? Daisy raced back to me as if to say she had no part in Walters accident, Nelly looked up from her ball and virtually said "serves him right" and Walter was down in the dirt. Come on Walts I'm not going back in the thistles today but oh yes I was... working on yesterday's technique of sliding on my tummy I rescued him but he was not for walking and no way could I carry. Eventually very hot and bothered we emerged from the bush and Walter has twisted his toe nail in the totally wrong direction and the nail is now sticking in the pad of the next toe. Making it quite clear he was a wounded soldier we, me, two dogs and a 'kangaroo' hopped home. I'm not sure what to do now obviously I can't pull it off as it's half attached and I'm hoping he bites it off although I do tell him off for biting his nails so I bet he won't. I can feel a vet trip coming on but then again is this an emergency????

Normality is back 'ish'.

One minute he is doing the dying swan act and next he is prancing about like a race horse on speed.

The initial plan was to just take the girls and leave Sir Walts to rest but that went out of the window... nipping upstairs to use the bathroom before I left, the tribe followed me as always. I did what I had to do and then walked to the landing stopping to apologise to Walts and explain that due to his poorly toe I felt it was best he have another day at home, he listened with his ears pricked. I turned round to come down the stairs and he literally jumped up and pushed me down.

Tumbling down three stairs and grabbing the hand rail for fun I turned round and I swear he was smiling ... ok you win!
Trotting down the main road like a possessed beast he was determined to show me he should not have been left at home yesterday. He literally was dragging me where ever he wanted to go.

Into the woods and Daisy, who has been very subdued since my kids moved out was released and off she went like a bullet only problem was she didn't come back, totally not like her. I loitered long enough for people to do the walk one way and then return and me still be standing there... odd... I blew my whistle and out she popped from a bush behind me ,I think she had been there all along! ... this was a fun filled day.

Through the woods- all good down Fairlawn and Nelly rolled her ball into a rabbit hole. No way was she leaving without it so another 10 minutes with her and then Daisy scrambling in a hole... they were clean until this point.

Mum my balls in here

Where?

Back through the woods and home, collars off at the front door and RELAX.... is it bed time yet?

Nice to be home

I'm not moving until I have to...

I am a total GOON....

Another beautiful sunny day and Walt's foot appears to be fine. I've waited almost a week before he has the opportunity to test it out and today is the day.

I threw the gang in the boot of the car and headed off to the beach, I checked the tide and it was out as far as it could be and there was not a sole about.... absolute heaven. We ambled, well I did. The gang raced and Nelly chased after her ball, it was perfect. Walter and Daisy did what dogs do and I picked it up in my little poo bag and placed it in the bag I carry with treats poo bags etc until we got back to shore and a bin.... Everyone happy and a lovely uneventful walk. Collecting the sandy ball and placing it in a bag to stop sand going on everything we rolled back. First bin, poo disposed of and into the car. Home and dogs washed, poor Daisy she really gets rolled in the dirt. Been sat in the garden for the past 3 hours with the door to the kitchen shut so 3 Sandy dogs can't leave a mess everywhere. Just come in and... my kitchen stinks .... I have thrown the ball away and put my little bag away full of poo.

Just when I thought I'd cracked a perfect walk .... NEVER.

Heaven...

The beach was totally deserted, it's like living on our own island and we all love it. The swallows were out in force and oh boy has Walter run today, closely (well actually not too closely as she couldn't keep up) by Daisy, Nelly couldn't be bothered and was happy to just chase her ball although she did have a little spurt. The tide was coming in and as always I wasn't paying attention and yep we got marooned on an island that resulted in us having to wade - me and Walts. Nelly and Daisy had to swim but still Nelly kept hold of her ball. Once we had crossed the ravine Walter collapsed in a heap ... he was bushed. Even the swallows who were trying to tease him by swooping in front of him couldn't tickle his fancy... he was bushed, however Duracell Daisy still had juice in her tank and off she went again.

Eventually we made it back to shore where I tipped out half the Atlantic from my wellies and wrung my socks out... nice. Once home it was hot showers all round and then we saw it-

Hubby has been very busy whilst we've been out he has built us an assault course to stimulate them..... not going to be easy they are all out for the count.

Gorgeous, Can't beat
a little paddle

Birds

And they're off

Daisy in full flight

Walts wait for me

54

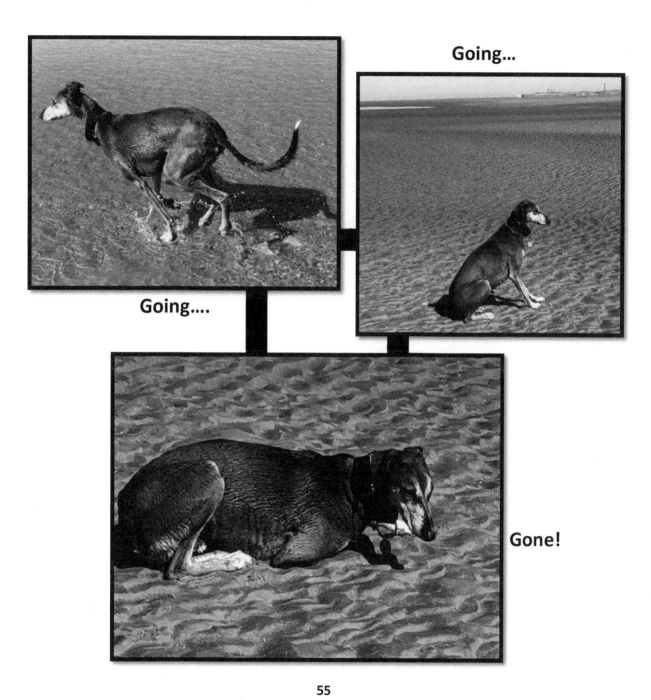

Going...

Going....

Gone!

Assault course

A magical moment.

I actually think the walk has been too much for the Amigos today.... Daisy fell asleep in her dinner, Walter has gone to bed and Nelly is unconscious too.

Knickers ....

We have had the most idyllic walk today. We set off early as it was very warm and Nelly is melting with her coat on, Daisy is my little ba ba black sheep and also very warm and for once Walt's teeth aren't chattering ... he's like me, loves the sun.

Through the woods and they were relatively quiet. Lately it's been horrendous with lots of people, dogs and bikes all chasing material but not today, thank fully.

I set off wearing a little skirt, a vest top and a cardigan not sure why but I soon took it off and thankfully tied it around my waist. I continued with the walk chatting to the odd person I saw (no they weren't odd just very few) and then back across the park where the gang met up with their mates but were too hot to race about, plus Walts still has a nasty sore on his leg that is a little weepy.... yesterday he went to every owner of all the other dogs in the group for sympathy.. he boycotted me ... it worked everyone gave him hugs and biscuits, Daisy followed him round for backup biscuits. Eventually home and thank goodness I wore/ tied my cardi round my waist. My skirt was tucked in my knickers and my wobbly backside was on full display .... phew! .... for once luck was on my side.

Blowing in the breeze....

We've been out today for a lovely walk. The park was empty and so were the woods but OMG the green and the beach were packed. The three Amigos desperate to get in the sea as they were all boiling especially

Nelly who at the moment looks like a Yeti. We walked along the path by the green and there's a shelter and from the shelter was (and please don't think I'm being inappropriate) wailing getting louder and louder. A group of about 20 people all in traditional dress were singing!.... me and the gang tried to distance ourselves but it wasn't easy as there were so many people. As we walked past I looked and saw two men pick up a little pot and throw its contents in the air.... Me, the girls and Walter were covered in someone's ashes. As much as I wanted to go 'errrr' and brush my clothes off I realised how disrespectful this would be so I waited until we dropped down on to the beach and then brushed dogs and me with gusto .... my little bag that I carry with poo bags treat and Nelly's ball was full of some poor persons remains... why would anyone want to stick on us ... must be mad. I have to be honest I've come home and washed the dogs and all my clothes.

Now she's taught him to do the washing up....

Finally I have a hair appointment today

Such a long day .....

They say things happen in 3's well I think we should have stayed in bed!.... my son borrowed my car and I needed dog food for Walts and the girls. Now the favourite is sardines and as hubby needed petrol too I said I will go to Lidl and you grab the petrol. Quick shop and hubby waiting in the car park, back in the car and home we go only the car was hopping like a kangaroo, suddenly! The air was blue... he had put unleaded in a diesel car.... thank God he did it not me.

Limping home I grabbed the leads and set off with the gang. No beach today as no car to get there so woods it would have to be. Busy busy busy.... with Walts and Nelly on leads and Daisy causing havoc we trundled along. Now today was all about Nelly, she must be giving off some sort of scent as loads of dogs were sniffing her which was a little unfair when they were off lead and she wasn't. I tolerated the extra attention she was getting but drew the line when a Pyrenean mountain dog tried to hump her and pinned her to the floor... trying to man handle this monstrous beast off her whilst it slobbered all over me was no mean feat and with the owner well in front of me oblivious to my dilemma I ended up shouting for them to remove their dog. Walts just stood and shook as he was a little nervous of this bear and if it had tried it on him I think he would of snapped. Daisy just sat in the bushes sniggering.

Out of the woods and along the edge of the green, finally some free time ball throwing and running was the order of the day. I opted to return through the woods rather than on the beach as all 3 Amigos were hot and with the shelter of the trees I thought it would be better for them- WRONG- a rabbit, a damn rabbit. Daisy and death seem to go together and despite the rabbit being safely tucked away behind a steel fence Daisy would not be beaten. Initially she was barking, incessant barking. Walts raced to see what all the noise was about and then he started crying too people were walking past but oh no my two were not for coming out of a huge prickly bush. Eventually after a good 10 minutes Walts got bored and appeared but nope not Daisy. Then the tone changed no longer was she barking she was screaming or was it the rabbit? I could stand it no longer I tied Nelly and Walter to a tree and climbed into the prickly bush getting badly stung in the process, Daisy the lovely Daisy was the one screaming and the damn rabbit was sat on the other side of the fence just watching her. Daisy had her head and one leg through the railings and was stuck, for God's sake Daisy. In a space the size of a shoe box and laying on my tummy I clipped her lead on but in the meantime I heard a someone say ' do you think these dogs have been abandoned they are tied to a tree'... I shouted "no they are mine I'm just rescuing my other one" they walked off ... thanks for your help.... carefully unpeeling Daisy's leg that enabled her head to be free we emerged from the bush. She is in disgrace.

Once home I appear to have had an allergic reaction to the stings and I am now on antihistamines as my legs and arms are covered in nettle stings....

I'm up, dressed, house tidy and ready for our walk.... where's the gang, oh yes! They are still sleeping ..... I'm not sure who these walks are for.

When you have to go to work and hubby makes your lunch and slips a note in.... hate him.

Where's Walter?

We've been out for dinner tonight to celebrate my daughters birthday, not everyone was impressed when we got home.

O M G
Designer boots

Don't use me to hide you

The sun is out.

I woke up early and as the sunshine was streaming through the window I decided to head out early.

The tide table is my bible and it said it would be high tide at 11am (it lied) so at 8:30am we set off for the beach. Everything was going great the birds were teasing Walts and Nelly and Daisy were happy running about. Then it all went horribly wrong!... The birds decided they were fed up of Walts chasing them so decided to migrate back to where ever they had come from, the only problem was, Walts went too and I lost him.

Now I know he often runs a long way off but today was different, very different, I actually lost him. Beginning to panic (a lot) I thought I was going to have to put 'Homeward Bound' rescue on high alert and get you lot on the beach to help me. Daisy in the meantime had found a new friend a dead duck and despite Walts being missing she was leaving him for no one. Nelly had her ball she was happy. I was having images of Walts being run over, causing accidents and generally being terrified on his own. Whistling, shouting nothing where's he gone. Walking back across the beach I spy him in the distance just leisurely strolling back towards me as if, "whats all the fuss about". Daisy delighted to see him wanted to introduce him to Derrick the duck, Walts wasn't too impressed, neither was Nelly. After lavishing cuddles and kisses on him ... I really thought I'd lost him I turned around at 10:10am to see the tide had come in.... my bible said 11am DAMN... gang we need to paddle AGAIN!!!.... Daisy do you really need to bring Derrick?

Finally back on dry land and heading for shore, Walter and Nelly on leads but nope Daisy refusing unless we bought the duck. No treats would entice her to leave it. Eventually she crumbled for a sausage, grabbing her collar and back on the lead she went but oh no that wasn't the end... as we walked past Derrick to say good bye Nelly sniffed it and Daisy went straight for the kill. Never, ever have I seen such a possessive dog for a dead Duck, poor Nelly just stood there as Daisy with teeth bared said "Touch Derrick and your dead..." all very embarrassing to poor Walts who just stood and waited for the girls to stop scrapping. Home by 11 and RELAX... Happy Sunday xx

Short walk ....

"Won't be long" I shouted to anyone who was listening, I don't think anyone was.

Me and the gang set off to a different location. In a similar area to where we usually go but we've never been to this exact spot and trust me we will never go again. It very nearly wasn't three Amigos coming home as Nelly almost drowned.

Walter and Daisy set off across the marshes skipping and jumping but when Nelly tried to follow it was almost a disaster!!! One minute she was skipping, the next she disappeared it was only when she started howling I realised she had a problem. Walking out across the marshes her little head was all I could see as she had fallen into a ditch and was totally submerged in gloopy mud and was sinking fast. She was panicking and so was I. The other two were on the other side of the ditch and still needed to get back over. Trying to reach her wasn't easy and I could actually see the whites of her eyes ....Thankfully Nelly is rather 'chunky' so I grabbed her fat around her head like a mother dog and with her crying because I was hurting her I yanked her out of the mud with a squelching noise.

Absolutely covered in mud and smelling foul her and I fell back onto the wet grass. She just stood there shaking and I was covered in mud too ...

I never wear trainers, jeans and a pale pink jumper and by the time our adventure was over we both look like we were in camouflage gear.

Shouting to the other two and telling them to "jump" or potentially Walts could have broken his legs and Daisy would have just vanished for ever they crossed the chasm.... yes, we've cleared 'Beechers Brook'.

We've been out for ever and all dogs are exhausted apart from Nelly who is traumatized and exhausted wrapped in Sophie's dressing gown.

Daisy day!

We HAVE NOT been out today as we felt it was safer for the environment plus the weather has been diabolical.

Over the past couple of days my family have been complaining that Daisy stinks I can't smell her (please don't worry I think it's because I spend so much time with her rather than covid symptoms) anyway I got so sick of everyone saying "Mum sort the dog out, she stinks" I took matters into my own hands... running her a lovely warm radox bath and warming the towels on the towel rail I spent 15 minutes trying to catch her.... knowing her fate she was dribbling wee in fear - yes I'm horrible to her so she had reason to fear me. Eventually catching her and carrying her up the stairs to the waiting bubble bath she was still dribbling on my hand and down my leg.

Plonk! In the bath she went and hang on she liked it... what a star, shampoo and bubbles, perfect. Rinsing with a cup she never moved a muscle. I actually think she enjoyed the one on one attention. Pulling the plug out and wrapping her up in a warm towel I rubbed and she shook, cheers I'm soaked now too. Opening the bathroom door and the other two were lining up for their turn, I'm not sure what Daisy said as she belted past them with her bum in the air and her head on the carpet but they all turned tail and belted down stairs.... at least one dog smells beautiful.

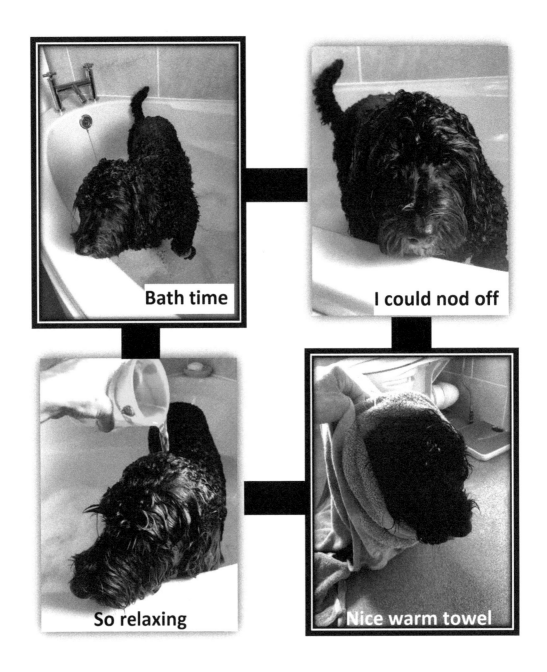

Bath time

I could nod off

So relaxing

Nice warm towel

The magic pink dressing gown.

Stupid or what!

We've been out on a very short walk today all because after a row with my hubby I said " how would you know what it's like going out with Walts you never come "..... he came with me today!!!!

We went to the beach.

Before we left I went in the bathroom, the Amigos came too. Shutting the door and sitting on the floor I virtually begged them to behave I should have known then from the glint in Daisy's eye she wouldn't.

In the car a very sombre affair, I don't think they liked the infiltrator and down the beach we went.... whats this 'Challenge Walts' day?...Labradors galore. Walts barking like a raving banshee, Daisy rolling on the floor trying to get off her lead and Nelly singing, it couldn't have gone worse.... hubby so not impressed.

Onto the beach and heading to the water through thick gloopy mud (his boots were filthy) Nelly happy with her ball. Walter very coy bringing up the rear but hang on where's Devil dog- oh no! She has found a dead seabird, inwardly I was begging her to leave it but oh no not her, the damn thing had to come the whole walk with us. Hubby saying "I thought you said Walts loved to run", maybe not today. I actually think he felt inhibited ....

Deciding this probably wasn't a good idea and hubby quiet the whole way we aborted the mission. Unfortunately Daisy didn't and categorically refused to leave the bird behind, nearing the car and still it was in her mouth, 'please Daisy give it up'.

Me and mate mate

Come on

 It's no good I'll ask have to ask hubby for assistance " creep up on her and grab her and I'll distract her" it worked but she was so annoyed that we'd tricked her, she is sulking now.

Hubby wasn't impressed either. I've told him I don't want him to come again so now we aren't speaking .... don't you just love this lock down lark.

I know I'm gorgeous...

Call us when the 'shrink' arrives.

Do you ever gabble when your nervous? That's me now.

I actually feel as though I have a social worker coming to check up on me (not that i ever had, so I'm not sure how I know what it feels like).

The house is spotless, the bathrooms gleaming and all surfaces are polished.... he's coming to see Walts not to see if I'm a contender for "four in a bed " the cushions are on the garden furniture and the coffee is on. Half an hour to go and Walts is smiling.... typical he hasn't smiled in weeks.

Smile

Dogs behaving badly.

Not really sure where to start on today but Wow!

The doorbell rang at 11am and Nelly started barking and screaming like she usually does, Daisy was racing around the house and Walter was jumping up and down like a kangaroo, not really knowing why but that's his input.

The man came in and completely ignored them all but they weren't for stopping so they ignored him and turned to me whereby I said "Nelly, Daisy, Walts calm down"... WRONG!!!! Craving attention and I gave it to them, first mistake.

He then went on to ask me some questions, to get a feel for the situation

1. Which room do they NOT have access too - oh they have the whole house.

2. Where do they sleep- My bed.

3. Do they ever sit on you on the sofa - Oh yes every night.

Before we can address other issues we need to sort home out first. Basically I am on the same level as them and until they respect me (nice if someone did) I will not sort ANY of the issues I have out....

We began by taking Nelly in the drive as that was a neutral space but

Walts and Daisy howled the house down it was so embarrassing, even my daughter, Soph said this is the worst I've ever heard. The man took Daisy out in the drive and basically let her know he'd take no messing. No raised voices, no harsh treatment just calm and incredible. Admittedly she was weeing everywhere but that was a minor.

Apparently Daisy is the catalyst for all the issues in this house as she is bonkers with oodles of energy and it's rubbing off on all the others. Until the gang accept that I am more important than them we can't move forward.

He is giving me two weeks to do my homework and implement major changes, no sleeping on the bed and no sofa cuddles until they have accepted me as BOSS then he will come out for a walk with Walts and bring his 40lb rotti (Walts will have heart failure) but I do actually trust him. I will probably have very little sleep tonight as I expect trouble with them being barred but who knows.

I have to instruct the whole family, we have to sing from the same hymn sheet otherwise it was a waste of time and money but I need everyone to know I AM BOSS .... I've always wanted to say that.

I took the gang out for a short walk this afternoon and they were model students let's hope this man can sort all my issues he believes he can and to be honest so do I ... I think I've found a gem.

Hmmmm.... first hurdle – FAILED!

Oh what a night.

Obviously you know I failed sort of …. initially I went to bed and told all 3 to stay on the landing. The dog man said leave my bedroom door open so they could see me. Whilst cleaning my teeth they all snook in and positioned themselves.. "No, you're not allowed out!" They all skunked out. Nelly was first to pop her head round the door, "no out" then Walts was crying on the landing so I got up to settle him which Daisy took as her cue to sneak on the bed. "No" my son then opened his door and said come "on my little black panther you can sleep with me "..... No Joe she isn't allowed, turning round both Walts and Nelly had got comfy on my bed, oh s**t. Night!

I have to ring the dog man at 8 tonight to tell him how my night went and I won't be lying when I say they DID NOT sleep on my bed. Nature is a wonderful thing, the ferocity of the thunder storm we had last night meant both Walts and Nelly lay UNDER my bed scared to death, what the dog man doesn't need to know was I was under there too trying to placate them both.

I totally want to try everything he has instructed but not sleeping with me when they always have is a step too far. However the other bits of advice do appear to be working. So far so good. Nelly now seems to spend her life on the naughty step.

With it being so warm we were up very early so off to the beach we went. Daisy's finds of the day were extremely impressive. Firstly she found a life belt, thankfully nobody was In it however when Nelly decided to go for a swim I thought we may need it... never seen Nelly properly swim I thought she was too fat and would sink ... sorry Nelly.

Next find was a quad bike, no person just a quad bike. Scouring the beach we couldn't see another sole - odd, very odd.

Then up on one of the poles in the sea we spotted a man. Not sure if he was scared of the dogs and had hidden up there or was working whatever we left him to it... just thought, I hope he wasn't going to jump off it!!

Home and showered and I have nipped to the shop, whereby on my return 2 barks and silence and three contented dogs .... I'm so pleased this man is working with me.

Relaxation

Mum's dead stressy today.
I barked and she told me to get on the naughty mat (I hate the 'dog man') anyway I'm hiding... I don't think she has seen me.

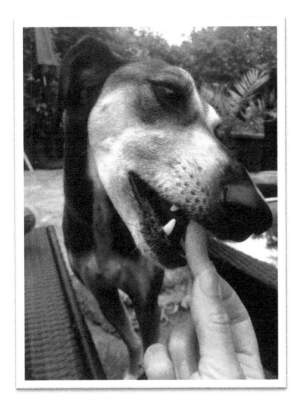

I'm not sure 'cheesy wotsits' are lurcher food.

SSSShhh......

It's been a very busy day.... I had to take the Amigos out early as my son was playing football this afternoon and there was a live stream on tv to enable me to watch. My hubby who is sunning himself in Cyprus phoned me just as we were off to the beach so being the proficient multi tasker I am, I put my phone under my chin and loaded the gang In the car, Preventing Daisy from stealing all the sausages in my bag.... with hubby still harping on about how he was struggling to download the app enabling him to watch the football we set off. Arriving at the beach and still my hubby was wittering through my hands free in the car I said, "I'm at the beach now I'll have to go" jumping out the car and I've got my slippers on, I've forgotten to put on my wellies. With Nelly's singing the worst ever we set off for home quick change and back to the beach.

Walters heart wasn't in it today and his preference was to lay in the sand with his legs in the air rolling. Daisy however was neck height in the water and Nelly was chasing her ball. Back home eventually and quick shower, unfortunately not as good as it should have been as my lounge has more sand than the beach does.

Lets all Roll

Get me out of here!

Back at work never mind the dogs having separation anxiety I do. I am seriously not enjoying being away from my gang. However at 1pm I was released and 'let the fun begin'.

I came home grabbed the leads and we were off. Fabulous walk through the woods and down the beach, the tide was coming in but still out far enough to enable us to have some fun.... Walter was extremely clingy at first and as Daisy and Nelly were careering about he stayed close to my side. Good excuse to keep stopping for a cuddle. Eventually the birds taunted him enough and he was off.... backwards and forwards along the shore line just what he needed.

We finally made it off the beach 15000 steps later or 60000 in dog steps I guess with four legs. Walter was bushed. Ok only thing for it, let's get an ice cream and relax.... I never eat junk food, sweets, biscuits or ice cream but I can't seem to stop. Laying on the green at Lytham surrounded by the gang and all sharing an ice cream ..... heaven.

Devil Dog Death wish.

Hubby came home last night from his hols and fortunately for me I was out with friends...

Knowing I was not going to be in he collected an Indian takeaway on route (I hate the smell), anyway the gang, obviously delighted to see him were going a little bonkers, apparently! A quick welcome home biscuit and hubby sat down with his curry, only for Devil dog to jump on his lap sending his tray flying and my lovely cream 'ish' lounge carpet is now sporting a large yellow stain... I'm surprised Daisy is still breathing.

Off to work and thankful to get out of the house when I get a phone call - hubby ...."The new tumble dryer is making a racket" - "is it?" I did actually know but can't tell him the truth. Daisy's name disk came off her lead yesterday when I was washing and drying it and the disk has somehow got inside the machine and is clanking away. I'll deal with that when the carpet issue has subsided.

Anyway today coming through the front door at 1pm I think the gang were more than delighted to see a 'friendly' face, hubby is Uber Uber grumpy. Jumping up and down and racing about it all got a bit giddy. Then Walter started screaming, he had jumped up and his claw had got stuck in the knit of my cardigan, for Gods sake what's the chances.... panicking he was desperately trying to detach himself from me but all he was doing was tearing my cardi... quickly taking it off he raced with my clothing still attached out into the garden .... I think it's ruined now I really liked it too. Let's just get out of the house - and breath.

Through the woods gorgeous and 3 clean dogs ... stupid stupid me " come on let's go on the sand" only it wasn't sand it was stinky, black, gloopy, mud . We all sunk... the gang were not impressed especially Walter... who doesn't do dirt ... Daisy does and was covered, Nelly definitely not impressed as her ball just sunk.

Home, hot shower and stacks of shampoo and still they smell and where's hubby STILL on his hands and knees scrubbing the carpet!

I'm sinking

Stinky

Can i stay on this Island?

Get off the Island

Happy Birthday.

It's hubby's birthday today, joy of joy... to say he has holiday blues is an understatement but to be fair coming home from a relaxing holiday to this mad house I'm surprised he's not got 'holiday blacks'.

It started early this morning. Nelly got a little excited when she saw him this morning and jumped on his lap expelling her anal glands all over his dressing gown ... disgusted and annoyed he got up leaving his unattended toast to get changed... fair game thought Daisy and ate his toast ... I was In the kitchen making my coffee.

The air was choice so to we hastily got changed and me and the gang went to the beach, beautiful. We never saw another person it was heaven. The girls were having a field day. The foam from the sea was thick so paddling was the order of the day but hang on where was Walts ... laying down and crying. "What's up"? He got up and stayed close to me, even Devil dog couldn't get him going today so no other option she'd have to race about on her own and he just stayed close to me.

When he did venture off it was towards the car he wasn't for staying out with us today.

Ok you win... come on girls we need to go home and guess what - he can't walk.

After a hot shower and a short lie down in the garden he can't move ... having a feel around his paw and leg as soon as I get to his elbow the scream escapes.... oh no!

Carrying him into the lounge as he really can't walk (such a pampered pooch) and pillow positioned to make him comfy not to mention giving him his piggy teddy it's another day in paradise.

Spoilt or what   **Me and my pig**

What a strange day.

Now I know you lot won't find this hard to believe but today has been a bit odd!

With the sun shining and me not having to go to work (I don't work Friday or Monday) me and the gang set off for the beach. Wearing a skirt instead of my normal trousers and a t shirt as it was so warm but still keeping the obligatory wellies we set off. The beach was packed but not on the area we were heading to. With Devil dog free of her lead and having stacks of fun the other two were still restrained as too many people and dogs... suddenly from nowhere came an Irish wolfhound or more like a donkey racing towards us... Daisy tried to protect us by barking but it just stood on her ... nope! It wanted to 'play' with Walts but Walter was scared and tried to charge at it. Angel dog also was getting quite het up too and the other dogs owners were miles away. Next thing... I'm on the floor, skirt above my head, knickers on show to the world but did I let go NO .. by this time the other couple were running (bit late now) but no damage done... I really must start to wear nicer underwear for dog walks.

Next test was Daisy - always Daisy, she found a dead bird but that got discarded when there were bigger fish to fry... we found a porpoise. Having rolled all over it they all stink. Hubby is playing golf this afternoon so before he left I phoned home... "please can you run a bath, the dogs have found a porpoise".... his response was " I'm warning you Des if you bring a Dolphin back to this house I'm leaving"... "No stupid the fish is dead the dogs are covered on blubber" .... what does he think I am?

Wow look at this Daisy

Part three of our day just got in and I've won the premium bonds £25 I'm 58 and only had my bond 56 years must be my lucky day!!!

All quiet on the western front.

Yes it's been very peaceful, uneventful and fabulous in the Riley household.

We've been in the woods during the week when most people are at work and then on the beach at the weekend. That way we have had oodles of space and no confrontations.... marvellous.

However -

3:17am this morning I almost had heart failure. I know the exact time thanks to the digital clock I have in my bedroom. Fast asleep ᶻᶻᶻ when suddenly a body flung itself across my face. Genuinely believing I was being attacked I squealed (pathetic really if it had been a real attack). Next I heard the jaws of death inches from my head chomp down... blimey was Walter going to eat me. Grabbing my touch lamp at the side of the bed Walter was by this time shaking on the floor at the bottom of my bed and I was shaking at the top. Slowly getting up I went to see what was up with him and why he'd lunged at me.... cuddles on the carpet and calm was restored. Back to bed and try as I may I couldn't get back to sleep .... why had he done that? Eventually I must have nodded off.

Up at 7am and it was as though nothing had happened or at least it was until I went to make my bed and there it was.... a Spider just above my pillow... squashed to my headboard. Walter had killed it.... basically he had saved my life In the night.

Oh bless him what a sweetie or at least I thought he was until I realised In his haste to protect me his clumsy big nailed feet had torn my bedding .... Oh well you can't win them all.

Tarantula

I saved mum's life

Hole in one.

What a beautiful day. Tons of squirrels around so Walts and Daisy were in their element. Racing through the trees leaping up and down and in 'Devil' dogs case putting into practice her party piece. She realised that she can use the ivy growing up the tree trunks as a ladder and scale part way up... bit like Tarzan in dog form ... fortunately no small furry critters were hurt in this process.

Nelly on the other hand was brought up with small furries so has no interest in any of them. Her only interest is her ball. She was happy to race after the ball and when we got down by the beach I chucked it and it vanished .... search as I did we couldn't find it anywhere, however Nelly categorically refused to move.... the damn ball must be somewhere nearby. Then I realised Nell was standing by a rabbit burrow... no way! I couldn't have thrown it into that tiny hole but guess what, I had. Reaching into the hole, a bit wary that I might come hand to face with an isolating rabbit but all good just Nelly's ball .... all smiles and eventually Nelly would move.

Back through the woods... the word was out, all squirrels took to the trees whilst the juvenile reprobates passed through ... home and yep you've guessed it ... relax. I'm loving this chilled out house hold.

Friends....

I have made a new friend this week and over time I feel our friendship has grown. He has stuck by me when Walter has categorically refused to come back due to squirrels, he has never judged me when my language has turned from pleasant to annoyed and today I spent an hour and a half leaning against him for support.... my friend is a TREE!

People with 'well behaved' dogs came into the woods did their walk and left, where was Walter, racing backwards and forwards like a total nutcase chasing b****y squirrels. Devil dog joined in for the most part but she is a delight, shake a treat bag, whistle and she is back sitting at my feet in a moment... hence her being obese. Nelly just sticks close because she is amazing and Walter goes into the 'zone' and I have no chance hence me making friends with my tree... I feel a bit like Shirley Valentine.

Yesterday I took them all to the beach but I realise based on today's performance that Walter should be in RADA. Obviously he didn't want to be on the beach so he feigned another injury ... bad leg! Crying, limping absolutely pathetic.... howling/singing to the radio all the way home. Sympathy all evening and then today back in the woods and right as rain.

Walter you really are a diva...

Angel dog

I'm injured - not

Fat girl

My friend

Rumbled...

Me and the gang set off this morning for our daily constitutional. With hip flask and blanket In tow, we set off for the woods. Walter was on fire it wasn't long before I wished I'd bought my pyjamas and a hot water bottle too. We were going nowhere fast.

Roll on the end of the squirrel season my patience is running thin. Daisy loves this manic lifestyle and despite being told she is obese she manages to sprint just as much as Walts. Nell on the other hand is quite content to lay in the mud with her ball.

Just when I thought things were coming to an end a film crew set up right in Walters line of sprint ... with very expensive camera equipment Walter was charging right towards them .. oh no! Just at the last minute the squirrel turned off up the tree, phew!

 I was totally unaware of 'fat' girl Daisy eating the sandwiches that were fair game on the picnic mat they were filming ... OMG only us.

Another 20 mins and Walter realised his partner in crime was grounded so he came back.... NO fun on your own.

Bit daft leaving cameras and Sandwiches unattended

Squirrels galore

Too much fun

ball & mud – what could be better

Home and I'm in the dog house ... Nothing new there. My hubby is going away on Thursday so I strategically planned a delivery for when he had gone.

He has made it clear that if I bring anymore animals home he's leaving, anyway last week I agreed to home hedgehogs.

We have done it in the past but we've had badly injured, brain damaged ones and it was quite stressful so we stopped but that was years ago. I have bought them a beautiful mansion and special bedding and ordered food that is gourmet to hedgehogs, but vile to us. Unfortunately that's where it's gone wrong. I arranged for everything to come Thursday but the food arrived today addressed to "Mr Riley".... why him? I ordered it. Of course he opened the box and 'hey ho' a bag of meal worms just what he's always wanted .. Guess what, we aren't speaking but never mind hedgehogs arrive next week .... You win some, you lose some, sorry Russ you lose!

Waifs and strays...

With the rain lashing down this morning the gang were not overly eager to go for a walk, however I was unable to go this afternoon as my son was playing football and I wanted to watch it. Walter with his jumper on BIG mistake I should have put his raincoat and wellies on. Nelly and Daisy a bit more hardcore went commando but were far from happy when it actually threw it down. We splashed across the park but I decided against the woods as Walter has been a nightmare with the squirrels recently, although saying that if they had

Can we go home Please

any sense they would stay indoors rather than be out in the vile weather. However we went down the front and along the sea shore.... Walter made it quite clear this was a walk he really didn't want to be on, ok you win we will go home.

Home and hot baths all round.... Walts hot shower in the garden then wrapped In my dressing gown. Nelly and Daisy upstairs to the bath... blimey how dirty were they, now it's just my bathroom that's filthy.

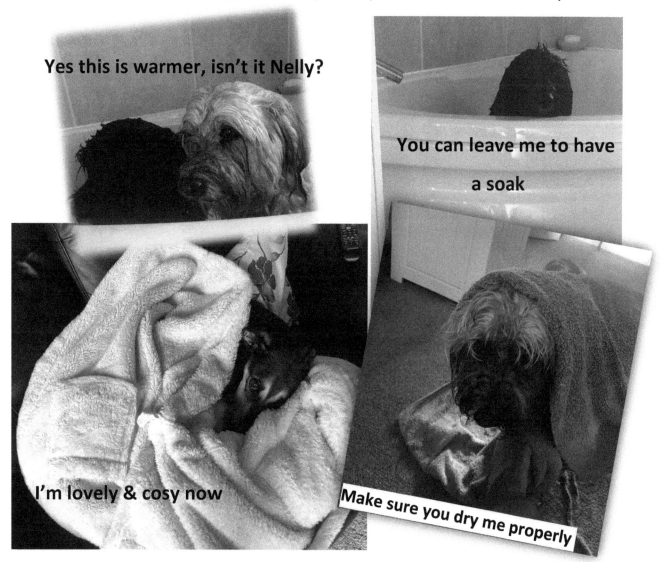

All because of the pyjamas.

No people, dogs, squirrels or small children, yes, we are in our 'happy' place, the beach.

As the girls both had a bath yesterday I opted to put their pyjamas on when we went out, anything to try and keep them clean. Walts was quite happy In his blue suit and the girls back in their 'pink ladies' outfits.

 I'm not sure what it is about Devil dogs Pj's but they seem to make her a bit 'fruity' only problem is the object of her affection is Nell... I'm guessing because she can't reach to do what she does to Nell with Walts.

Poor little Nelly was jumped on at every given moment and all she wanted to do was chase her ball. This was the sequence... I throw the ball, Nelly races after it. Daisy chases Nelly. Nelly jumps on the ball, Daisy jumps on Nelly.

I know there is sibling rivalry but when Daisy took it a bit far and almost drowned Nell I had to step in.... Where was Walter? He was stood on the waters edge sunbathing, totally oblivious.

Drown Nelly!

Beach heaven

Taking in the rays

Nelly's pyjamas don't have legs in the back as she doesn't like them so when Daisy mounted her and pushed her into the sea the water and sand easily got inside her suit thus making it very heavy and baggy... poor old Nell couldn't get up she was stuck. Daisy was almost laughing at this point and to add insult to injury ran off with her ball. Basically I had to peel Nelly's pyjamas over her head and tip all sand and sea out by which time she was filthy... cheers Devil dog!

With the sun shining and not too cold we meandered back to the car.... three happy dogs and a very happy owner. Life is good!

Full of sand and water

What do you mean it's raining and we aren't going out

The Riley household are feeling very lazy today...Walter just wants to find his spot on the settee, sorry Joe!

Cordon bleu.

Anyone of a similar age to me will remember Wendy Craig in 'Butterflies'... the Mum who was a dreadful cook .... that's me.

It's Joes birthday today so being the goon I am I was up early and a cooked breakfast was the order of the day. He ate it all .... or so I thought.

Fast forward an hour and me and the gang set off for the beach, Nelly's legs seem a lot better and I know she desperately wanted to join us, so off we go. Nothing unusual in Nelly singing on the journey but Walter joined in too... how lovely everyone singing carols .... WRONG!... arriving at the beach I opened the boot of the car to find out Walter hadn't been singing 'away in a manger' he had actually been throwing up and to make matters worse it was the breakfast I'd made Joe.

Now if I'm ever sick the last thing I want to do is race up and down on the beach but Walts is obviously different he was more than happy.

And we're off

Nelly was in paradise, she had a new ball Chucka and her legs seem to have held up quite well. The occasional seaweed bed she found made a comfy resting place whilst the other two nutters raced about.

I'll just lie here

I phoned ahead and asked Joe to run the girls a bath, 3 times I rang but he didn't pick up, good job it wasn't an emergency. Eventually he rang me back, he was on his PlayStation and didn't hear the Phone, anyway he put the plug in the bath and a splash of Radox (muscle soak added for Nelly).

I'm not poorly!!

Arriving home I went to rinse the worst of the sand off in the garden but the water pressure was very low, oh no! he's gone back on his stupid game and forgotten to turn the bath off... Without removing my Uber muddy wellies I raced through the house chanting a mantra ... "please don't be overflowing, please don't be overflowing" ... phew! almost at the top, Joeeeeee .... 'oh yes I forgot it' ... I can't shout, it's his birthday. Placing the girls in the bath and how dirty were they.... they are both sat shivering in the lounge watching a Christmas movie with their pyjamas on and the heating... good job hubby away.

Night!

How dirty

Radox time

Devil dog .... WALTER!

Yes you heard me right. He has been a pain today - still love him though.
I'd promised to take my Mum out for a little treat so a quick walk was the order of the day. Ha! Who am I kidding. Across the park which was very wet and very muddy and into the woods. Daisy off, Walter off and Nelly close by (not too bothered with her ball today) a man who we see regularly walked past "morning" I said, "morning" he replied "are you alright" I asked "NO" he said.

We just happened to be near a bench so we sat together, I know distancing and all that but he needed company. We chatted, we laughed, he was lonely. 40 minutes we talked and the dogs just caused mayhem.... where was my therapy dog when I needed him, actually that was a very

good point where was Walts. Leaving the man, hopefully a little more cheerful we set off In Search of The 'legend'.... Daisy was happily chasing squirrels and 'knock knees Nelly was getting slower and slower behind me. We were meant to be on a quick walk, this was all going wrong. In the distance I saw our lovely boy but just behind him was a little boy probably about 4 years old chasing him. I whistled Walts and he stopped dead and the little boy grabbed his tail Walts was off like a bullet. Oh no! By this time Nelly had had enough and was laying in the dirt.... trying to entice her up I pulled the treats out of my pocket only for Daisy to appear as if by magic and throw herself at me. Oh no! my new coat absolutely filthy but more importantly where was Walts... picking Nelly up ... she is such a lump we trekked after his lordship.... Eventually catching up with him sitting at a bench I usually sit at waiting for him... role reversal by this time we had been out for absolutely ages. Poor Nelly was so weary and her joints were clicking, you could hear them.

Daisy was just happy leaping up the trees and fences desperately trying to catch a squirrel and Walts was grounded .... another day tomorrow GOD HELP US!!!!!

Come on Daisy lets play

I've been good today

My legs are aching can we go home

Naked.

I didn't get the dreaded phone call from work today so this morning we cuddled and then the three Amigos relaxed on my bed whilst I hoovered, dusted and polished. My grumpy hubby was upstairs in my sons room building furniture that I had ordered from IKEA... I had to shut the door as I didn't want my gang learning new words that were being banded

around upstairs. Deciding the safest option was to leave the vicinity we togged up in pyjamas and set off.

Crikey it was a cold one today.

All good so far across the park and into the woods. Daisy is a little cagey with a bad back but much better than she was. Suddenly! a squirrel appeared right under Walt's nose, he was off sprinting as fast as he could and Daisy was in close pursuit (lovely to see her run again). Smiling to myself me and Nell carried on. Then came the scream oh no! What has Daisy done now ? I bet it's her back. Wrong!... she had leapt obviously for the squirrel and somehow impaled herself on a tree branch by her pyjamas. Wriggling but stuck suddenly the material gave way and she was free - with legs flapping in the breeze she was off

I enticed her back and tried to refit but it was hopeless no alternative she had to go naked.... stuffing her 'Jamas' in my bag, Nelly looked so cheesed off, she hates wearing hers and I could see her eyeing up the nearest tree to rip hers on. Walts on the other hand was shivering like a jelly and needed to get home to the warm radiator.

Mum I've torn my Jamas

What time are we going out?

I can't believe he is
sucking his thumb

Free to a good home (or any home!!!)

Walter is either suffering with terrible twos (although we know he is older than that), adolescent anger, or just male moaning (I'm surrounded by that).

Let's start at the beginning - he has found his voice.... if he wants to go to bed he barks, if he wants to go out in the garden, he barks (happy with that one) if Daisy has his favourite pink pig, he barks, if the girls sit next to me on the settee he barks, BE QUIET!!! Just when I thought he was an Angel he has, with his partner in crime, learnt to open doors. I make the bed in the morning he opens the door and him and Daisy jump on it.

Then yesterday we went for a walk with our friend Sue. Nelly stayed at home with stiff joints. I took charge of Daisy and I handed over the reins of Walts .... I was off duty. So despite warning Sue that he would chase the on coming golden retriever I just carried on walking whilst she ran to retrieve her charge. Heading into Lytham we decided on a hot chocolate. I stood In the queue and Sue and Walts stood to one side suddenly Walts lunged at the 'pain au chocolate' that was sitting on the counter, fortunately quick reflexes prevented a theft, but I'm sure he must have slobbered on some poor unsuspecting persons breakfast .. making a hasty exit we headed off for home. Then last night the barking commenced again only this time he was sitting in the kitchen. Oh for goodness sake I had just made myself a coffee and sat down with my treat of all times.... M&S white chocolate cookies. Getting up to let him out in the garden but NO he changed his mind, however Nelly needed a wee so she went out and he went in the lounge, next Daisy needed a wee, oh great! my coffee will be stone cold. Eventually the girls came in and I returned to the lounge and guess what - Walts had sat and chomped his way through a whole packet of M&S finest .... all my b****y biscuits. When did this sweet tooth fetish begin?

Then today oh today up early all out in the garden for their ablutions, plenty of rain last night so lovely and muddy. Whilst drying Nelly's toes on the towel I keep near the back door the other two made a run for it opened my bedroom door and used my bed as a trampoline- great! Only changed the sheets yesterday and now look, anyway, out for a walk down the beach and woosh! Off he goes and yep! You've guessed it, he found a sheep, I knew as soon as I saw him trying to drag it - oh no not again!!!.... Daisy not wanting to miss out raced over to her mate, Nelly wasn't interested whistling Walts who basically said "get lost" as did Daisy. Trekking over to them, me and Nell waded through the marshes. With wool hanging from his mouth and Daisy playing catch me if you can I retrieved them both and phoned the council - I was 12 in the queue, patiently waiting I got to position 2 when I was cut off.......aaarrrgghhh!!

Home safely and Look .... butter wouldn't melt.

We are meant to be 2 metres apart

Thanks Nell for lending me your jumper... it's more like a crop top on me

What a beautiful day ... unless you're an eel ....

With a good tide we set off to the beach and the gang were released. Initially the Walk was a bit gloopy but trekking through the sludgy mud we soon made it to the lovely sand. Heading out to sea and the gang were all playing nicely. Walts was chasing Milo (A temporary member of the gang) Rosie (Our friend Sues dog and a weekly addition to the gang!) was chasing Nelly and Nelly was chasing her ball... nothing new there but where was Daisy.... turning round Daisy had something in her mouth.... long and thin and worse still wriggling. Screeching at Daisy to drop it but knowing the more I screamed the more determined she would be to hang onto it (remember Dennis duck)?

Calmly walking over to her with my heart pounding I tricked her with a treat to drop the critter.... it was an eel, it was thrashing about on the sand and a long way from any water so I had no alternative but to pick it up.... I'm not too brave with fish and I've seen films about conga eels how they bite.... I don't think it was a conga but just my luck to lose my arm.

With all the dogs in a frenzy, I ditched Nelly's ball and chucka and set off in search of the sea.

The eel was wriggling for fun it was a horrible sensation and I didn't want to crush him so I only had a gentle hold on it... suddenly the killer of the group Milo leapt up and snatched it out of my hand, "MILO".....
screaming at him to drop it eventually he did and the poor little, although

to be fair I don't think it was that little, thing was still wriggling.... I had to get it back to the water and quick.... like the pied piper Me, 5 dogs and Edith eel set off.... Eventually wading in to the water as far as my wellies would allow, only Walts could keep up with me we released Edith .... fortunately Walter is a lover not a hater so he was happy to see me release her although she sank straight to the bottom.... not sure if that what eels do or if it had all been too much for her.... I know it had for me.

Walking back across the beach to retrieve the ball and chucka and to put a smile on Nelly and Rosies face we set off for home ... 3 hours later.... everyone is asleep now .... A good positive day though, unless your name is Edith eel.

Hanky panky.

I have had to return to work but only for the interim and to be honest my heart isn't in it, so at 1 pm when I was released I virtually ran home .... the gang were waiting!

Across the park 3 lurchers and a Labrador, this could be fun. Releasing Walts and the girls and the race began. Flying around the field all playing lovely together even the Labrador didn't phase Walts today. Through the woods and empty again. I love this new take on life. Everyone crammed into restaurants, bars and cafes and me and the gang in complete isolation. Next was the sand dunes...

Oh dear God why ?.... a couple decided to lay right in the middle of our dog walk.... unfortunately I didn't see the small plate of sandwiches or the cake stand balanced on the floor next to them all I spotted was two people fast asleep on the floor. Unfortunately Daisy and Walts spotted them too and off they charged.... Walts leapt over the woman on the floor, knocking over the cake stand whilst Daisy, his partner in crime legged it with the sandwiches. Obviously they woke the people up in the melee but hey that didn't stop Daisy.... she was off, nobody was taking her corn beef sandwich from her. Apologising profusely but the couple weren't bothered they had finished..... clean up then you goons don't just go to sleep.

Next to the beach and everyone happy. The tide was in so lots of paddling and plenty of fun to be had on their boat .... All aboard.

Abandon ship !

Looks like engine trouble

Captain always leaves last

My Lap dog.

After making a spectacle of himself on the foreshore and racing backwards and forwards chasing the birds he eventually returned to me, Nell and Daisy. we had sat down on the sand to wait for him to finish. A number of people walking along the prom stopped to watch him in full flight - it's a joy to behold. However he stubbed his toe, oh goodness you'd have thought he'd broken his leg .... such a baby but a beautiful baby.

Cuddles from Mum though made everything better

Police incident.

I'm an advocate for Primark knickers but occasionally the shearing elastic dangles and tickles your legs, it's so annoying. I therefore knew exactly how Walts felt today, don't worry he wasn't wearing Primark knickers, although it won't be the first time.

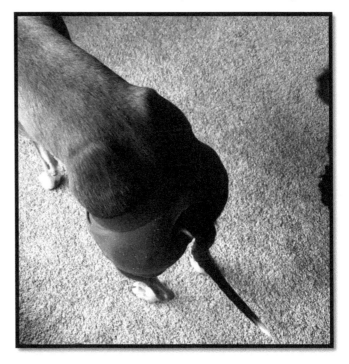

We set off on what was to be a nice 'clean' walk.... the gang were pampered yesterday and the girls had a hair cut.... I was so jealous. Not only did they look beautiful but they smelt divine too, no way were they going to get dirty on today's walk.

Across the park and through the woods, so far so good then down to the sand dunes but not in the sea. Just our luck! We arrived at the sand dunes at exactly the same time as two mounted police - Daisy went out of her way to get arrested, barking, pulling and desperate to chase the horses. I kept all three dogs on a lead to prevent a situation. With the horses plodding in front of us and Walts dragging behind suddenly! He collapsed in a heap and started to throw himself around the floor, what on earth .... initially I thought he was fitting but thankfully nothing so serious. He had a cotton that was tickling him and being the drama queen he is he was desperate to distance himself from it. Daisy in the mean time was also rolling but unlike Walts she was soooo content. The horses had left a steaming pile of dung and she was making the most of it. She doesn't smell too good now. Angel dog Nelly just stood waiting to continue with our walk away from horses and poo somewhere safe to throw her ball.... another day in paradise.

Divas......

Knowing how spoilt the Amigos are I decided they needed new garden furniture. The donuts that we have in the house have been absolutely brilliant so I opted for three of those. Now the in-house ones are huge, big enough for all three to lay in so i pain stakingly measured, first the girls, two beds at 80cm each and then for the big boy I bought a 100cm one. Obviously I told hubby it was buy two get the dearest free .... they cost a fortune but In his eyes well worth £30 for 3!!!

Anyway in the pouring rain they arrived today and my kitchen is awash with donuts .... Daisy has claimed the biggest one, smallest dog biggest bed, Walts is perched on the small one with his head hanging over the side and Nelly would prefer to lie on the stairs rather than any hairy bed Fussy or what.

Big dog little bed | Little dog big bed | Whats the fuss about

After a stressful day this was Walts.

When I was little my favourite book was 'princess and the pea' - the wicked queen placed a pea under lots of mattresses and to see if the girl was a true princess only she would be able to feel it through them all .... seeing Walts balanced on a tower of donuts reminded me of this story- obviously he is a true prince.

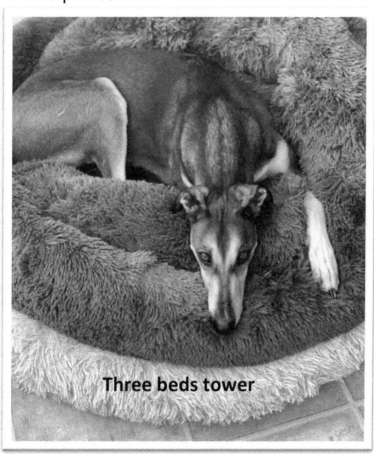

Three beds tower

Who needs an umbrella?

Albert.

Who said rescuing a hedgehog would be a good idea. Releasing Albert into the great outdoors once it went to dusk seemed like a good idea - WRONG!.... the Amigos took it upon themselves to make themselves known to him and come hell or high water they were not for coming back in the house. Daisy raced around the garden with her nose stuck to the floor, Walter just galloped around the garden chasing Daisy and Nelly sat on the patio howling, bit like a whale does when it's calling it's young.... my neighbours must hate me.

Grabbing leads and collars I dragged the gang back in doors and Alfred was able to search for bugs in peace, or at least that is what he thought. 1:30am hubby was up as he was going away and Daisy having run all over my sons white bedding with her dirty shoes on was banished from his room ... running down stairs and barking which woke the other two all three were at the back door, before I had chance to shout 'don't let them out.' They were released and of course all they really wanted was Albert.

Russ had to leave, so yep! I was left to round up the troops, it took a fair bit of time and I hadn't once seen Albert.

Eventually we all fell into bed (me and the gang, not Albert).

We've all been weary today thanks
To Albert. Walts found a reliable
pillow when we went out for a
hot chocolate

I really need to top up my tan

You just couldn't write it ....

We were later than usual going out for a walk as I had a funeral to attend this morning. After a sad morning a walk with the gang in the sunshine was just what the doctor ordered. The park was extremely busy, a complete contrast to the woods thank goodness.... I've learnt I don't do people.

Everything was good. 3 happy Amigos, when suddenly 2 ladies appeared with four very large dogs.... Walts was extremely intimidated and with his tail between his legs he scooted out of the way. Walking on he composed himself and his tail reappeared- all was good in "Waltie" world. Leaving the woods and heading to the sand dunes again it was relatively quiet. All dogs released and Nelly happily chasing her ball or at least she was UNTIL...

I threw the ball and it landed on a small hollow a few feet in front of us. Nell raced as always to retrieve it but squealed and ran off. Suddenly a swarm of wasps appeared... OMG .... I had thrown the ball In a wasps nest and we were being chased... Walts was half way to Mexico and Nell and Daisy were just rubbing their noses along the floor... there were hundreds of the damn things. Eventually calming Walts down I opted to leave the dunes and go back into the shade of the woods - great plan

5 minutes in and the women with the 4 big dogs reappeared and the dogs made a bee line for Walts again... this time Walts became submissive sat down and shook. The women called their dogs but they ignored them, they called again and eventually they went to them. I wrapped my arms around Walts to reassure him when suddenly a large branch just in front of us snapped off and a child fell out of the tree... I didn't even know there was a child up the tree but he belonged to one of the women with the 4 dogs.... Walts was off.... he was stopping for nobody. Daisy thought this was a great game and went too and as far as the child I guess he survived I didn't hang about to find out. Walts stopped when I blew my whistle and lay down .... we're home now and I tell you a day in the life of ..... I promise you this is all true.

Ps all measures in place to make Walts home a fly proof den and then we find a wasps nest!!!!!

My spin on things.

3 years ago Walter was a feral dog, beaten, hungry and broken. I'm guessing used as a coursing dog to chase small furries and kept in vile conditions hence his fear of insects and flies. I could be wrong on all counts.

However -

Roll on a few years ... He is now a highly respected member of the local community. Takes the lion's share of a king size bed and absolutely adores cocktail hour when the crisps are out
Walts your world has definitely changed.

Celebrity status

Better than sleeping rough

Crisps and cocktails

Feet in the starting blocks.

Gazing out of my office window I decided to take the gang to the beach when I finished at 1pm.... Cold sea and a breeze, lovely. Arriving about 1:30 and being ignorant to other cultures I just saw a large group of people all in white flowing robes and one man sat slightly away from them with his back to the rest, I presumed they had fallen out with him and he was sulking - WRONG!

Suddenly he started wailing as did the other people. I hadn't taken Walts off his lead at this point and Nelly is glued to me until I throw her ball, but Devil dog had heard the commotion and was off. Omg she was heading into a praying situation, shouting my favourite word 'chipolatas' she stopped, thought for a moment - food or jumping over crisp white outfits, thank God or Allah or whoever, sausages won.

The beach was idyllic. Empty apart from the birds that the gang love to chase, Nelly just looks on in disgust and me listening to music actually singing, as I said at least nobody else was about.

Spotting a large colony of birds I knew that Walts and his side kick would be off in no time and yes I was right. Racing as though he was in the 'arc de triumph' with Daisy on his tail well maybe not that close but having a good go to keep up. He had a real good run to burn up some energy all three are now snoring particularly loudly outside in the garden. If my neighbours think it's me snoring ᶻᶻᶻ I will be carted off to the doctors... what a Racket All very happy though and I feel better too.

Can this day get any better 3 tins of sardines for tea followed by cheesy wotsits - isn't that the staple diet of a street dog?

Come on you lot, get up! I've got to go to work.

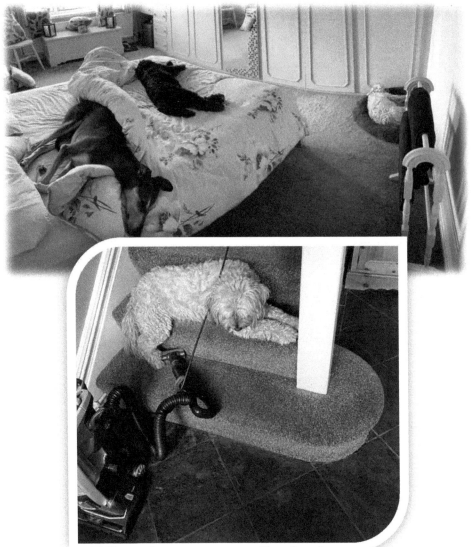

What do you mean I'm in the way.

Let's have a blast at the sea side and that's exactly what we've had….

Taking the Amigos to the beach with the obligatory ball we set off. As is the norm for us it was deserted so everyone happy. We'd been out about 15 minutes when I threw the ball for Nelly and off she belted. Now Nelly has this habit of placing her ball at the top of a mound and letting it role then chasing it however she did this today and it hit the water bobbing away from her. With the tide going out it was moving away quite quickly so I went to the rescue, wading into the water fixated on the ball and not the height of the water it was a bit of a shock when I suddenly felt my wellies filling with sea water. Turning back towards the bank I realised my feet had sunk in the sand and I toppled over great just b*****y great! Grabbing my bag I managed to save my phone from getting wet but not me I was soaked and where was Daisy, my little hero had swam out grabbed the ball and was waiting for a biscuit once I'd composed myself.

Now do I turn back or, carry on? Dripping, I decided to carry on. Probably not the best idea as my wellies were rubbing as were my wet trousers but can't let the gang down.

Continuing to throw the ball, Nelly was happy and Daisy and Walts were in full flight with the birds. Suddenly Walts went on a mad one and ran and ran and ran until he was so far out of sight I was getting a bit twitchy. Me and the girls waited and waited but no Walts just great! We started to head back towards the direction he'd run in when I saw him limping, oh no! Limping back to us…. NOW WHAT? He was feral for a while, injury free - moved in with me and everyday he has a new wound but this one is nasty. He has obviously gashed his leg on something- Daisy taking this as her cue to get the upper hand leapt on him to which he crumbled in a heap … even she looked worried. Taking it easy and with my inner thighs chafing we headed back to shore and the car. Eventually loading each of the gang in they were set for home, me on the other hand squeezed into the car and removed my soaking wet trousers after all nobody could see me. I am such a goon I got to the car park barrier and didn't get close enough to slip my ticket in. I'd have to back up and try again… noooo somebody has pulled up behind me, Oh God! I will have to get out of the car and I've no trousers on plus the barrier is next to the ice cream hut that had a queue of people.

I had no choice knickers on display ….
Only ever when I'm wearing Primark, never Victoria secrets (I actually don't own them) and I've flashed to the town.

We're home now before we are arrested …. I've dressed Walt's leg but he preferred to rip it off and go digging in the mud so now I've masking taped a flannel to his leg …. This dog is a total liability but I adore the bones of him.

Sanitise.

I'm doing a volunteer job at the moment at the school I retired from last week!!!

I went to work at 8am today and was home by 9 so everyone, including me is thoroughly confused with my work pattern. However home by 9 meant i could take the gang out for a nice early long wander.

The lazy bunch hadn't even finished their breakfast when i came back but as soon as they saw the scruffs come out of the wardrobe they guessed they were on for a walk. Nelly racing around the house like a nutter screaming. Daisy laying on the settee waiting for calm and Walts jumping up and down like a kangaroo but not having any idea why.

Leads on and we were off. Across the park where Daisy loves to chase the sky larks who tease her for fun. Nelly happy to run after her ball and Walts just mooching. All is good and still its not 9:30am - I like this life.

Through the woods and it was empty and this is where Nelly sanitised me. Throwing the ball and Nelly chasing it, just as i caught her up she dropped the ball to the floor. I bent down to pick it up but it had rolled under her tummy so i thought grabbing it through her back legs would be the easy option and it would have been, if she hadn't squatted and weed all over my hand …. Great! Flicking the majority off i realised my sleeve was soggy too, thanks a bunch!

Where theres one theres two

Continuing on, chuckling we dropped down onto the beach - great i can wash my fingers, the tide was in but so were a few jelly fish …. Daisy be careful, they are not edible.

Opting for the ladies that do lunch routine me and the stinky gang went for a hot chocolate. I love my new life.

Next was a romp in the long grass, wherever Walts goes a little black dog is close on his heels…. Now relaxing at home. Daisy on my bed, Walts in the garden and Nelly in the armchair… what a great life.

And it's still not lunchtime

Just chilling

Night zzzzzz

Wheres the sun

Life of Riley

Why me…
I've got conjunctivitis, I'm lame on my right leg and I'm fed up… the vets said I've to have horrible drops in my eyes. And I've to be on bed rest for 3 weeks …. Is he mad?

A slightly different turn of events today....

As the weather was warming up I opted to take the gang out this morning. Now bearing in mind Daisy is on bed rest it should have been only Nelly and Walter who went out, Haha not a chance. Daisy made it quite clear that if I didn't take her too she was going to do some serious damage.... I had a quiet word in her ear that she could come provided she took it slowly, she agreed. Once I released her lead she was off like a bullet - she lied.

Regardless of her fibs we had a lovely relaxing walk and all three couldn't have been better behaved, yes even I was shocked.

Arriving home and life was good. Sitting down with my three babies on my lap and my book in hand we settled for a nice lazy afternoon (hubby at golf, perfect).

Fox party.

I'm absolutely loving this volunteer lark…. I went to work at 8am and by 8.30 I was home again, my days work completed.
The Amigos totally overwhelmed to have me home so quickly showed their appreciation by scratching all my legs and peeing on the floor, that's actually Daisy she gets over excited.

Giving all the school kids chance to get to school - I live in the middle of three schools we relaxed in the garden- hubby works on Tuesdays and Fridays so today we have peace, perfect.

By 9 am the gang were ready for the off. Across the park bliss, empty!…. Through the woods, again empty, love everyone else working.

Then on to the sand dunes where I bumped into my friend Carol who is a dog Walker with the biggest black lab I've ever seen. Hmmm this could be fun…. Obviously Walts made the obligatory rumble but this tank wasn't phased, next Walter is in the let's play bow stage and game on…. The two of them charging about like maniacs. Daisy who shouldn't even have been out with us (you try leaving devil dog home alone) was more fixated with the other dog Carol had a Weimaraner who was actually scared of Daisy - I get that, she scares me sometimes and Nell was just happy with her ball.

All was good until the lab decided he was going to try and hump Walts. At that point Carol stepped in and put him on a lead and Walts charged back to me as if to say 'did you see what he tried to do' we dropped down on to the beach to continue our lovely walk. Nelly running after her ball and the other two just pottering UNTIL- all 3 stopped what they were doing, noses in the air and they were off... out into the marshes and omg there must have been one heck of a foxtrot going on last night because all 3 of them reappeared covered in fox poo . Now I'm fortunate as I can smell nothing (apparently I had covid, I didn't know. Antibody test confirmed and I have no smell or taste) how lucky am I today?

At the end of our walk we set off through Lytham and our favourite hot chocolate cafe was empty ... we made a bee line for it. Ordered and got a large bowl of water for the gang.... They drank the lot. A couple then came and sat down. The whole place empty and they sat right next to me Suddenly just as my drink arrived the man said - excuse me is it you that smells!!!!!

What do I say to that? I said I hope not, I think it's the dogs to which he said "They stink" .... We left my drink and departed, nobody tells me my gang smell, even if they do.

Showers given or rather bubble baths - the gang not impressed and then I know let's all lay on Mum soaking wet. I've actually missed a bit on Walt's head but no way will he go back in the bath.

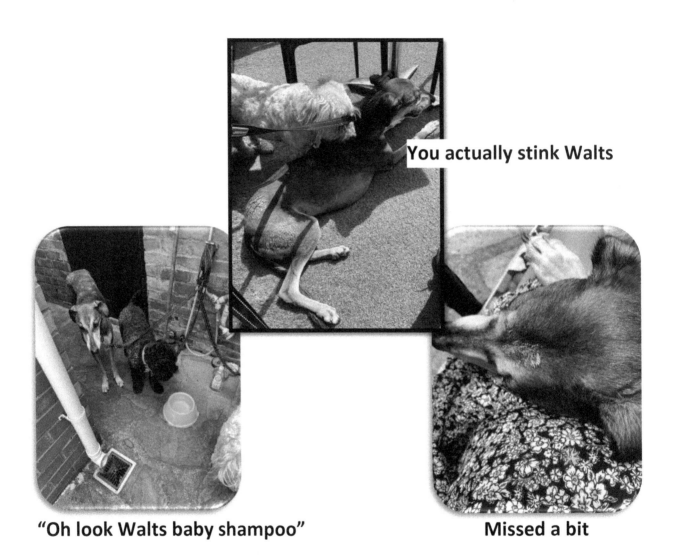

You actually stink Walts

"Oh look Walts baby shampoo"

Missed a bit

How can that be comfy?

Nobody puts baby in the corner.

Ok Daisy your allowed to come out today but only for fresh air, no walking …. Haha… who am I kidding. Brainwave last night, I will use the pram to push Daisy and the other two can run and she can watch. Collars on, leads attached and the chariot in place in the kitchen. Loading her highness in, she looked a little unsure but I'm sure she will be fine. Clipping her in so she is safe I turned round to put Walt's muzzle on - Suddenly! She leapt out panicked as she was attached to the pram, tipped the pram over and off she raced, dragging the pram behind her, knocking over kitchen chairs, plants and causing total carnage…. Walts belted upstairs out of the way and Nell just stood and watched with a perplexed look on her face.

Hubby was not impressed and just said "told you it was a dumb idea". Not one to be beaten I picked up the debris and wheeled the pram out of the front door. Placing her back inside and grabbing her lead we set off…. We made it to the garden gate and she did it again… jumped out and pulled the pram over. Walts bucking like a bronco and Nell just laughing …. Ok you win but don't blame me if you can't walk later …. Home, soaked, filthy and guess what – limping.

Liar!

I purchased a 3 metre parasol for the garden to go with my new cushion covers and new dog beds... yes my garden will look smart this year.

As Daisy is still limping we opted for a relaxing afternoon sat reading my book and chilling, especially as hubby is playing golf.

Now Walts prefers the 2 seater settee to the floor so before he left hubby put the umbrella up so he wouldn't get too hot.

Daisy was happy on the floor - life was good but then - this is the "life of Riley" we are talking about!!!

Out of nowhere a gust of wind took the umbrella and the weighted base on the ride of its life and it toppled on top of Walts who was dozing.

Daisy in her panic spray weed everywhere including the plate my melon was on and bolted down the garden.

Walts was like a rat in a sack, legs sticking out from everywhere... I was out of my chair faster than Usain Bolt. He is fine nothing that a brandy won't put right.

The parasol on the other hand is not too healthy and is now laid to rest – RIP.

I know hubby won't be cross as at £20 it was a bargain!!!!…. That will teach me to tell fibs.

All that remains

Brandy works a treat

The adventures continue...

Thanks for following me

About the author

Derren Leweson grew up in Lytham St Annes before marrying her long suffering husband Russell and taking on the name of RILEY.

She is Mum to Sophie and Joe and her fur babies Nelly, Daisy and Walter. Part time she works in a local school but her true passion is animals. When Sophie and Joe left home last year it caused 'Empty Nest' syndrome so, only one thing for it – Derren threw herself into animal rescue. With fear etched on his face and trepidation in his heart Russell awaits the next addition to push him further down the pecking order.

Welcome to the "**Life of Riley**".

Lightning Source UK Ltd.
Milton Keynes UK
UKHW050941061121
393492UK00003B/39